Becoming Water

HEART PATH TO WISDOM:

Poems on Life, Love, and Awakening

CAYCE HOWE

A
Zen Z Press
Publication

zenzpress

Printed in the United States of America

First Printing, 2019

ISBN: 978-0-578-21097-1

Book Design by Kory Kirby

Graphic Design and Art by Cayce Howe

DEDICATION

To the infinitely available sweet taste of freedom that resides within.

To Katie, my fiancé, a living embodiment of said freedom.

CONTENTS

FOREWORD

I am delighted that Cayce asked me to write this foreword to his book, *Becoming Water*. I have known Cayce for nearly 15 years, as a dear friend and Dharma student, and he never ceases to amaze me. Among his many talents that continue to reveal themselves to me, I had no idea that writing such beautiful poetry was one of them.

Cayce's poetry has the feel of words that come from his deep contemplative experience and realization. In reading them, I am reminded of the poetry and songs of realization of so many of the great mystics of the world's wisdom traditions: the *dohas*, or sacred songs, of Saraha, the Indian mahasiddha; the poetry of the great Sufi mystics like Hafiz and Rumi; the writings of the Beguines of northern Europe in the Middle Ages. These poems have the very same freshness and immediacy. They obviously arise out of direct experience, and not out of mere intellectual understanding.

This small volume contains deep wisdom in addition to inspiration, in lines like "I look forward to the funerals for the versions of myself I long to let pass" and "If you never practice being where you are, you will never notice when you have arrived." "Be careful where you set the bar for happiness – suffering is everything beneath it." Each stanza could be used as the basis for meditative contemplation.

May this volume of poetry guide you, the reader, into your own deep insights and understanding, and lead the way to liberation.

VEN. TENZIN CHOGKYI
Soquel, CA
11 July 2019

BECOMING WATER

If I throw a lit match at you, and you are combustible,
a fire is inevitable.

If I throw a lit match at you, and instead, you are
water, what happens?

Life will throw everything from embers to
flames your way, ready to set you ablaze.

This you can't control.
What is in your domain is what meets that fire.

Once the attention is shifted away from the arsonist
outside, an inner realization can be seen.
You notice that your essence is water and always has
been.

The next time life serves you up a forest fire, you can
stand in the middle of it, cool and calm like a deep
mountain pool. The fire stays at the edges,
never a threat to your primordial stillness.

Life

Be your own muse.

The only way to suffer
is to believe a
suffering thought.

Wisdom is tuition-free—
The professor is your own guiding heart,
the lectures are the dynamic play of life,
and graduation never comes.

Work and play are even in the
realm of being-ness.

My laundry used to be done every Sunday,
but now my hamper is overflowing.

Yet, I have poems on paper,
paint on my hands,
and a dirty motorcycle in the garage.

My next goal is to let the grass grow long.

Passion for life is not acquired through
empty breaths on wishful clouds.

It is a courtship propelled by equal
forces—you and destiny.

You must yell through the cavernous unknowns
to behold your echo of truth.

You must be blinded by fervent prayer
before the kinship of purpose is united.

The train of destiny never slows.
Speed up, match its pace, and leap aboard.

Creativity is a conversation
held in the corridor
between the known
and the unknown.

Disappointment needs two
opposing forces—
how it is, and how you want it to be.

The moment, however, is singular;
it has no choice but to accept itself.

Believe in your own light and shine.

Be careful when trying to get
ahead that you don't
leave yourself behind.

Let us unravel together,
surrendering to the earth's atonement.

Water will cleanse.
Fire will burn.
Wind will clear.
Soil will transform.
The Great Mother will show us her passageway
home.

What if we are actors in our own play, temporarily forgetting the vast expanse of our limitless freedom so we can experience an embrace, a tear, a triumph, a tragedy?

What if the things we are striving for are not nearly as important as the experience of striving?

What if the very things we wish to let go are the very things we have come to taste?

What if we were to surrender to this experience in our totality?

What if?

Peace is a subtraction problem.

We cannot will something away.
We cannot anger something away.
Whatever we push away, we feed.
Only when something is shown love is it
free to go.
In the process we free ourselves.

Follow someone who tells you to follow yourself.

You do not need to be easily
defined, labeled, and consumed.

May they never figure you out.

The wild play in the curiosity lying past the
edge of normal.

No need to avoid yourself.

You're going to find yourself out sooner or later.

Better to be blunt. Have a sit-down heart to heart chat. Fight it out if you must.

Have a good cry.

Just be sure to end with a hug.

Even if we wanted to, is it even possible to fully
absorb a single moment of this wonderment?
But we do want to—we do want to feel fully, love
fully, LIVE fully.

The heart knows this. It is holding our hand
through the forest of bewilderment. It is lighting
the dark path ahead. It can remember eternity. It
is eternity—the spark of the infinite.

We can follow our hearts into the heavenly now.
We can follow it right back to what we have been
looking for all along—to be the experience of life.

This is it. Looking out from behind your eyes is a
being that desperately wants to be. It wants to be
this—

Just. This.

We pay money to watch a movie for hours
 but may have difficulty looking within for 20
minutes.

Take time to befriend yourself. It will be the
greatest love story you will ever know.

Success is failure gone wrong.

Why build a home in the ego
that can be blown apart by the
winds of life, when in the
basement of your being lies an
unshakeable soul of jewels?

Be careful not to confuse boredom with peace.

Thoughts don't have
teeth.

Emotions cannot
cut you like a knife.

Let the great I AM
tame them in the boundless yoga of
space.

Scaling the flames as my inner hell rages,
I reach the soft heavens.

I trust that in this moment I have
everything I need.

There is absolutely nothing lacking;
There is nothing insufficient.

Still, I move as if there is something to gain;
not because it will make me happier,
but because I'm a full expression of dynamic life.

And life moves all on its own.

I'm here sitting with
the universe,
talking with its' creatures,
inhaling… exhaling.

Loosen what is
binding the mind, and
the knots of life will
untie themselves.

Failure is forgetting that
the finish line still lies
ahead.

A relationship is like two plants
sharing the same pot—
each person adding their own nourishment or
toxicity to the soil.

A commitment to wisdom and kindness
will have you both in bloom,
strong and beautiful,
for the whole world to admire.

I have decided to be perfectly ok
with how things are, while I actively
engage to shift the things that need
shifting.

You are a birthless, deathless,
indestructible love particle—
existing as an universal power source.

Not only capable of transmuting
the foundational elements of all creation
into an individualized conceptual "Self," but
capable of understanding yourself as a
myriad of realities simultaneously.

So don't believe them when they tell you
to measure success on a smaller waist size,
a bigger house, and a face without wrinkles.

I look forward to
the funerals
for the versions of
myself
I long to let pass.

There is something achingly mysterious,
that a being will emerge from the cosmic dust,
carrying an invisible divine spark,
leap into an earthly life,
do things unimaginably great and utterly mundane,
only to resend the invitation,
extract itself from the human cage,
and disperse once more
to navigate the celestial seas.

How can one not be in a suspended state of awe?

We tie the mind in knots,
wondering why it is tied in knots.

When something captivates you, it is
not time that stands still,

it is the cessation of craving.

It's ok.
You're ok.
In fact, there is nothing wrong with you.
Nothing.
Really, I mean it.

Nothing.

Attention is the ultimate currency.
Be sure to spend it wisely.

Nothing real is predictable.

A thought's true nature is to
fade away—
your true nature is to let it.

True courage is being with the
totality of your being—
ghosts, demons, angels, and saints...

all of it.

You can ask the universe
for what you want,
but
it won't work any harder than
you do to make that happen.

If you never practice being where you are,
you will never notice when you have
arrived.

The mind is a navigation system.

Make sure it is pointed
in the right direction.

Be careful where you set the
bar for happiness—
suffering is everything
beneath it.

Only in freefall do we realize we are the sky.

Wealth and Lust
are optional, Love
and Compassion
are not.

Your life's purpose is
something that you fail
at, but love so much
you keep doing it
anyway.

Be wary of those who
speak too loudly.
Truth can shatter eons of doubt
with a mere whisper.

The secret to hard work is
mastering the art of rest.

Trust in the effortless.

The best things are found when
we stop looking.

Understanding
leads to knowing
like forgetting
leads to being.

Inward I ran
through a mind humming like busy downtown
traffic.

I continued on until my feet slowed to a jog as
thoughts became lazy, like an evening walk down
a country road.

Mother Nature's pace was then at hand,
I sat, letting the mystery swallow me whole.

Those that follow live in a world that is already built, for those that lead, there is no end to the possibilities.

Love

I'm here to love.

I walk through the
world in awe at how
many ways love can
say, "I love you" to itself.

Troubled is this mind,
constantly choosing between
a body in fear,
fighting to survive
and a spirit in love,
that knows only immortality.

On the threshold of surrender,
I followed the Wizard's eyes.

The mind had long ago rebelled.
If there was to be a journey home,
only the heart was left to wind
the sails.

The only sanity
is to be insane
with compassion.

The path
is
love,
and the
path is
now.

Grandson was talking to his Grandmother
Love and Grandfather Wisdom.

He asked,
"Grandfather, what is your most sage
advice?"

Grandfather answered,
"Listen to your Grandmother."

If you can love what is here now,
there is no need to look
for future liberation.

We love
because that's
what we are.

In every drop of kindness lies
the blueprint of awakening.

Kindness is a seed. Like a seed, it carries with it all the intelligence it needs to bear fruit—in this case, the fruit of realization. There is no act of kindness that does not carry with it the fruit of our highest human potentiality.

As kindness grows, it becomes self-nourishing. With every act, it becomes stronger. Dividing lines begin to disappear. First to slip away are the obvious ones—race, religion, gender. Then come the more subtle divisions. People that we once saw as enemies start to emerge as kinsmen, just another being acting out of the shared suffering we all experience.

We begin to disappear.

Kindness becomes a wild crop, popping up unplanted, sometimes unwanted. It is compulsive, and its reasoning is far from reasonable. We feed from it, instead of it feeding on us. We become a lowly pollinator drunk on the nectar from a unseen blossom of kindness.

We see the parched tortured summers of drought in the eyes of passers-by, and watch as kindness gathers the clouds, and with magical rains, gives life to itself once again.

Love is inexhaustible to those
with no desire to control or
contain it.

If you are chasing love,
you are chasing
yourself.

May the fire of compassion burn away the illusion of separateness until the luminous clarity of heart-mind blazes as one's sole reality.

Love was sitting next to a young man one day.
Love turned to him and asked, "In all the world,
what is the one thing that you long for?"
The young man turned to love, and answered,
"I don't know; my desires seem to change daily.
Sometimes I cannot keep up with them. I know that
whatever it is I want, I have not found it yet."
The young man then returned the question to love,
"What is it for you? What is it that you long for?"
Love closed her eyes. A single tear wet her check.
She then began to laugh, opened her eyes, and
spoke.
"You see, I am longing. I know nothing but longing.
Longing is my service, my gift, and my beloved."
She continued, "when I asked you what you longed
for, I was not speaking about your cravings-what
you desired.
I was asking to know what tears you apart? What
causes you to ache, to crumble? What is it that you
will give your life for?
If you are to find this my dear, you will find what
you have been looking for".

Beware of compassion.
She is a thief.
She stole my prized
possessions of fear, jealousy,
and hatred.
Now I'm left writing love letters
on the hearts of strangers.

I'm dating the love in my own heart.

Sometimes we get in fights, and I give her the cold shoulder.

Sometimes I sit with her with undivided attention as the hours slip by.

I cannot get enough of her story of how she came to be.

Sometimes we meet with friends, and sometimes I go places without her. But as I fall deeper in love, I notice that when she is there, it is always a better time.

Lately, I have wondered if her love is true. I think she may be cheating on me. I have started to see her with others.

At first, this concerned me, but then I thought, "her love is so beautiful, untamed and free; to limit her, would be to destroy her."

Instead, I have begun to welcome the sight of her, however she chooses to express herself. Lo and behold, we are getting along better than ever.

I'm thinking, "she might be the one."

Love towards something may bring out the best in
you, but it can also bring out the worst.

A deeper love is objectless.
It lies there beating,
radiating out,
touching without discrimination
all that flows through its field of influence without
a source or destination.

True romance is with
the playwright,
yet all too often we are caught
in character,
trying to catch the sunshine
and fight off shadows.

A blanket and some food can outdo the world's most beautiful love poem.

Dear One,

The love you feel from another is your reflection
being mirrored back to you.

You are love, as a mountain is a mountain,
no one can give you this or take it away.

If a mountain forgets, it sees its reflection in the
lake below,
but it has never ceased to be a mountain.

You may see your reflection in another's eyes, but
love you can never cease to be.

Imagine the new worlds that await discovery
when our eyes see
what only the heart now beholds.

Love is the openness that
replaces control with the
desire to understand.

With a single kind gesture,
 a poetic peacefulness
can fill our being.

We see how the heart sees—
the illusion of separateness fades
as does the craving to self-feed.

Instead,
our heart becomes incandescent
as it yells through the tears,
shouting across dimensions
a new message of freedom.

The message is surrender—
surrender to the wounds,
to the laughter,
and most of all…
to love itself.

Compassion without the Wisdom of
Emptiness turns to attachment.

The Wisdom of Emptiness without
Compassion turns to nihilism.

With both wings strong and balanced,
the bird will fly true towards the Great
Sun of Enlightenment.

Release limitations,
separateness,
mortality.

Love will catch you.

There is a woman like no other,
and a dog,
and a cat,
and a home.
And when the furnace broke,
we never once felt cold.

Build an empire of love, complete with a love fortress and an army of love to overpower ignorance, build a factory of love built by machines made of love, build love on top of love, have a National Love Day, and every day is National Love Day, create jobs for people to create more love and employ other people to tell them what an amazing job they are doing, that they are loved, have sporting events to see who can "out love" one another.

Let a dog rule the empire—as an example of the unconditioned state of love, pave the streets with love and drive cars that run on love, light the streets with love and when the lights dim hold gatherings of love to empower their return.

Build an empire of love. Today.

We cannot wait any longer.

Only those that love fully can see fully.

Invest in others
and the universe
will invest in you.

Awakening

Better to wake from the dream and face the truth,
than spend a lifetime building fantasy.

I'm a devotee of something I cannot see, hear, taste or smell, and yet is so real, it renders the senses false.

More of something that is empty is still empty.

I saw a place where we were free.
You were there.
We were free.
We were free.

The path is a circle.
We keep running into
ourselves asking,
"How much further?"

Nestled in the sweet
bungalow of introversion,
a sage found opulence
through a mind free of confusion.

Now is the only Now.

There is no other Now.
No past or future Now,
no better or worse
Now.

To know the Now,
know yourself as the
Now.

There is nothing to lose.

This life is eternity
blinking her eyes,
a momentary release
from the burden of timelessness.

A repose into the finite.

Rest in the small quiet space of individuality
because next time you awaken,
it will be into the arms
of everything.

No longer am I a being molded by suffering,
for I awoke as the cast builder.

That which is looking
at sadness is not sad.

That which is seeking peace
is already at peace.

What you are seeking
is non-seeking mind.

When there is nothing to do, do nothing.

On the parched desert floor of longing,
where strength is an empty shelf and
doors without a handle at every turn.

When even doubt is dismissed as fiction,
only then is the creature coaxed through
the needle head,
and pierced into wildness—
freeing the hell fires to rage
tall enough to walk atop the tips
and into heaven's embrace.

Wisdom
is hidden
in the vault
of silence.

Desperately
we seek
to learn
what can't be taught.

The path to bliss is a long,
arduous journey,
where you end up
right where you started,
but with a wiser heart
that is happy to be home.

The philosopher goes mad for truth
as the wind whispers,
the clouds shade,
and the watering hole gives.

The warrior's final
test is to summon
the courage to be
nothing.

There is no source. Nothing
has ever left anything to
become anything. What you
see in front of you is nothing
more than a room full of
mirrors.

We are like a droplet in a small stream paying homage to the mountain peak for birthing our existence, forgetting that we have evaporated into the clouds, and given birth to ourselves.

So often there is doubt. Yet, there is no teacher, no book, and no teaching that can show you, YOU. You already are what you are seeking; the failure to remember this takes one on a journey away from the destination. Eventually the hunt ends up dry, finding only treasure chests empty of jewels.

Dejected, but now closer than you think, you walk back into yourself. It's an odd place, quiet, and vacant at times, and then boisterous and unnerving. It's not love at first sight, it's better—deeper.

The desire to know more leads to exploring more, and eventually BEING more. Connection now becomes a living presence, no longer made up of a list of social get-togethers but as an entity, breathing alongside you, within you. Not only that, but the mountains in the far distance share the same breath; so do the streams that run down their face, and the animals that drink the waters.

There you are, with the entirety of yourself—equal parts human, earth, breath, spirit, life, death, and everything in between. And you haven't moved a muscle.

Truth is that which is left unimagined.

Remember: You wisely cached provisions for this crazy human adventure inside yourself.

The head of the lineage is
awareness itself.

The root guru is compassion.

The practice instruction is
to leave things as they are.

A saint is a con putting on an ego,
and meeting us in delusion,
only to reveal us both as frauds.

I watched the thought as it
pressed its way towards the
awaiting mind,
landing with a tender ease…

Then watched the reverberation of its
birth make its way through the
universe in a momentary eternity.

I'd rather be
awake in hell
than asleep
in heaven.

Space can hold a trillion stars without effort.

Much like this, our infinite
compassionate awareness can hold
our thoughts, emotions, and body sensations
with ease.

They arise in our sky-like mind,
but never once does the sky think it's the storm.

A leaf is neither resilient nor fragile.
When it meets the breeze, it simply moves. When
the breeze calms, the leaf calms.
When it is time to fall, it falls with grace.

Throw away your beliefs, throw away your ideologies, your prized character traits—that "life of the party" charisma, your best body feature, those beautifully sculpted thighs. Throw away what got you here—to this paragraph…this sentence… this word, to this epiphany of the moment.

Throw away hope that it will get better because you are wiser; throw away the fear that it can all be lost. Throw away the first of your ideas; throw away the latest attachment to the best version of you. Throw them all away.

Throw them into the still night of the soul—the one that has been bartering for your freedom since the dawn of your conscious choice—the one that has been begging you at every intersection, for you to lean into the unknown with the fearless courage of one who knows that beyond concept lies that which can never be destroyed.

Throw away the choice, and the choice maker. Pull out the rocking chair, take a seat. Look at the view…you are done.

Surrender may be the only thing left to do—the only thing to do in the first place.

A life of ease is a life of surrender.

This does not mean lifeless, or passionless. On the contrary, surrender is to find that beauty is here—that there is both a pregnancy, and a fruition, and death all here to be recognized in each moment of conscious awareness.

Surrender is letting go of the battle for more—for better, for when I get the raise, when I retire, when the kids grow up. Surrender is the deep breath, the sad ache of loneliness, the spark of hope, the pain of rejection.

To move with surrender is to move with the sun, wind, and rain—it is to move with yourself.

Truth is slow, still even.
You cannot speed up and catch it;
You must be still, and let it find you.
Once it does, you can never outrun it.

I am the light forgotten.
You have called me soul, spirit, essence.
Yet, I cannot be conjured into something fixed.
Beyond the edges of comprehension is where I lie
in wait, patiently calling for your return,
my heart sons and daughters.
You have been traveling throughout spheres of
material existence,
so that we may find every last expression of love.
Together we have danced throughout the eternal
night in the magical display.
Look into the eyes of that which you love,
and it is I that will return your gaze.
Merge with me by letting yourself be unearthed by
love at every opportunity.
Walk as if you are floating. Speak as if each word
is a song.
Live like there is nothing lacking, and share as if
you own the world.
There is nothing that I will not do for you, but you
do not need me.
 I am the flame, but you are the light, sparkling
in timeless myriads throughout the manifested
planes.
You are so close to the light, you have forgotten
what you are.
My dear, set fire to the fear that binds you.
Set yourself ablaze and let your light be known.

On desolate roads I have wandered
through centuries of war and peace.
Like a drunkard, happy and ignorant, I have
plundered away my divinity on the crumbs of
human cravings.

That is, until the kiss that killed me.

The darkness closed in on the periphery as love
hurled its way through the ancient hallways of
my being.
I lay cradled in her wail of forgiveness.

I grasped at the primordial static of delusion, yet
its veil had been pulled.

She was everywhere. She was everything.

The wise seek not to know the words of
truth's song,
but to be carried away by its melody.

This world is but a bubble on the infinite ocean of consciousness.

Looking outward, we see our little bubble.
Looking inward, we fall into the sea.

Hidden behind what I think I know, truth awaits.

You are not your beliefs—you are the
love that is freed once you let them go.

Wondrous the abodes on
the outskirts of ordinary reality,
where the divine is both
sustenance and currency.

I don't know any-thing
because there is always some-thing new.

So I have surrendered into no-thing,
curled in the womb,
where mother silence holds me near.

We can readily find fear,
but in countless lifetimes
fail to find the "I"
it was sent to protect.

In a mind with no fields and no fences, we build imaginary boundaries.

Surrender to the heart, and we can run forever.

When I was in the world of worlds,
courage howled on the stinging winds,
and summoned terror from the depths.

Of the wrath that followed,
I have not a memory.

For my heart swallowed whole
the hate of old,
leaving my alchemized eyes
suffused with rapture
and a will devoted to servitude.

There has never been an adventure more perilous and more worthwhile than the pilgrimage back to yourself.

Glorious is the day when
sandcastles of the mind yield
to the ocean of truth.

Awareness is the firm ground of existence,
yet we grasp onto sinking ships
in imaginary waters.

The vast expanse of my being
will no longer fit into
the box of conformity.

Look within not to escape the world,
but to put it in its rightful place—
a phenomenon arising and disappearing
against the backdrop of infinity.

A crowded mind is a soul's cage.

There is no more.

The experience of getting
is inside of you;
needing an outside trigger
is an illusion.

Mind the mind in devoted stillness,
and you will find it all there—
a ripe fruit in a secret garden grove.

How do you convince a wolf
that has walked too long in sheep's
clothing
that it can feed itself with its fangs and
claws,
and that its howl can lead it back to its
ancient den?

The best things are found when
we stop looking.

Throw away the map,
the journey,
the destination,
you have arrived long ago.

Air laced with the sweet grace of devotion,
holy men with sweat on the brow
and chests yearning with reverence,
hoping to coax her ever closer to their beating
hearts.

She asks but a single sacrament be kept—
to leave alone what one does not need.

And to that end, the cleansing winds
lift gently the egoic encasement.

One by one, they fall into her arms,
golden, and not a piece left misunderstood.

To best describe oneself,
leave out the description.

Equal to the extent
I adorn this moment,
is my ignorance of its
innate resplendence.

Cease to look beyond the now,
and jewels once hidden
appear like a ship emerging
from a morning fog.

A kaleidoscope of interlaced dimensions
harmonize,
boasting the presence of magical things like
sky, water, humans, leaves, ideas, sounds,
objects…
All in agreement with time to create a
"moment."
This art will vanish upon arising, never in
eternity to be seen again.

What if it's all perfect?

Life moves fast, awareness does not move at all.

The Dharma is not here to give you anything, it is a reminder that you don't need anything.

One's greatest
accomplishment is to
realize there is nothing
to accomplish.

ACKNOWLEDGMENTS

I would like to acknowledge all my teachers, including Venerable Tenzin Chogkyi and the entire InsightLA Long Beach Sangha and fellow teachers. You are family.

I would like to acknowledge the retreat centers and communities that have given me so much: Sunburst Sanctuary, Land of Medicine Buddha, and the Vajrapani Institute.

I would like to acknowledge my retreat masters Khenpo Jigme and Lama Wandu for creating a wisdom filled container.

And last but not least; my Mom Debra, and Dad Frank. Whom both beautifully embody infinite love.

ABOUT THE AUTHOR

Cayce Howe is a Senior Meditation instructor for InsightLA. He also teaches private clients, facilitates workshops and retreats in the United States and abroad. He teaches through his art, poetry, reflective writing, and wisdom talks.

Cayce's meditation practice has spanned over 25 years and has included living and working for nearly six years at meditation centers, mostly in the Tibetan Buddhist tradition.

His other passions include a lifelong addiction to motorcycles, and hanging out with his two rescue animals, Mala the Siamese kitty, and Wolfie, a scrappy terrier mutt.

PLEASE SAY HELLO

I would love to connect with you!

Visit website for blog, event schedule, and podcasts:
www.caycehowe.com

Email: cayce@caycehowe.com

Instagram: @caycehowe

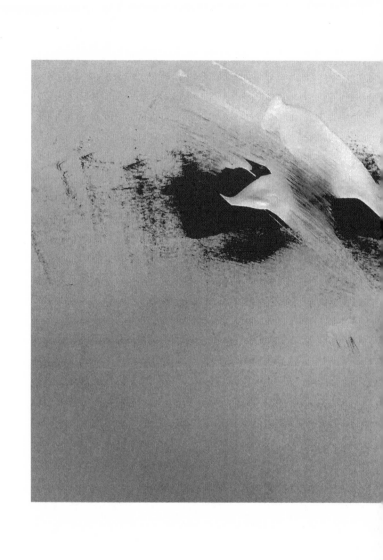

Made in the USA
Middletown, DE
23 April 2021